All His Gifts

Love, Life, Loss

God Bless You !

James L. Cartee

All His Gifts

Love, Life, Loss

James L. Cartee III

Light Messages
Torchflame Books

Durham, NC

Copyright © 2021 James L. Cartee III
All His Gifts: Love, Life, Loss
James L. Cartee III
www.daddydestinations.com
jamescarteeiii@gmail.com

Published 2021, by Torchflame Books
an Imprint of Light Messages Publishing
www.lightmessages.com
Durham, NC 27713 USA
SAN: 920-9298

Paperback ISBN: 978-1-61153-437-5
E-book ISBN: 978-1-61153-438-2

Book Cover Art by Teri McLaren tetonvalleylocalart.com
Copyright © 2021 Teri McLaren

Special thanks to Teri McLaren for the use of her
painting on the cover. Enjoy and support Teri's art at
tetonvalleylocalart.com

For Lisa,
my Better Half

PRAISE FOR *ALL HIS GIFTS: LOVE, LIFE, LOSS*

"When I first met James at The Christian Alliance for Orphans Summit, he was generous and kind, and I have seen James grow both as a person and writer since that first meeting. His writing is honest, and the sacrificial love he has for his wife, Lisa, is evident. Love prevails in the face of adversity, and James's love is raw as he agonizes through depression and failures to express the feelings we all face in life. I relate to his creativity, and I am convinced all readers will feel his expressions on a deeply personal and relevant level as I have."

—John Sowers, Ph.D.,
Author of *The Heroic Path and Fatherless Generation*

"Stephen King described writing as refined thinking. If that is true, then poetry must be refined feeling. Christian poetry is considered by some to be a lost art, but in *All His Gifts: Love, Life, Loss*, James Cartee bares his soul without an ounce of self-consciousness through this moving collection of southern fried slam poetry. This time-jumping collection touches on everyday themes experienced in life by all readers. I felt the pain, sorrow, and happiness of the author in his personal walk with Christ, and, for a brief moment, I even knew what it was like to be James Cartee."

—Justin Gabriel,
Author of *Kings of the Promised Land*

"'Life is not a problem to be solved, but a reality to be experienced' says Soren Kierkegaard. The living of life is seasoned by times of pain, joy, betrayal, loss, and love. James Cartee opens his heart and mind, inviting his readers along his intimate journey as he explores the path God laid before him. Throughout, he celebrates the good and bad, the ugly and beautiful moments. With his words, he weaves a tapestry of human existence, reminding us all that heartbroken tears and the heart-skipping beat of love-at-first-sight exist seconds away from each other. His message rings true and clear. Though the path may be bumpy, God stays with us on the ride, offering his great gifts of love, hope, and rest in Him."

—Donna Mumma, B.A.E., M.Ed,
Writer

"In *All His Gifts: Love, Life, Loss*, James Cartee explores themes that are intrinsically related to the longings and questions of any human heart, regardless of creed or age: the quest to be known and accepted and loved as we are. With life's many setbacks and disappointments, James dives deep into his own personal search for meaning while suffering, eventually arriving at the joy, hope, and purpose that only an active God that raised the dead to life can provide. These lines elucidate St. Paul's certainty in that 'all things—even our suffering—work together for the good of those who love the Lord and are called according to His purpose.' James has responded to the call and is inviting his readers to tag along in our journey home."

—Kevin Okseniuk, M.S.,
Engineer

"I had the great fortune of meeting James on a hiking trip a few years ago. For both of us, hiking is a spiritual adventure, connecting with God in a unique and powerful way by immersing ourselves amidst His awe-inspiring creation. As we exchanged photos from our trails, I caught a glimpse into the mind and soul of James Cartee, and after only a few photos, I felt like I had known James for a lifetime. Every photo depicts a powerful story, motivated by a soul driven to inspire, from a heart that bleeds to glorify God in every breath and every step. His imagery captures the essence of a moment while revealing his inner character. His technique cleverly personifies his struggles, doubts, and fears while celebrating his jubilant times with others. His eyes and words are a lens into his soul.

As a clinician, I have learned to appreciate the power of the human psyche as it strives to process the multitude of thoughts and feelings that bombard our lives daily. For many, however, the trials and tribulations James has endured are overwhelming. Yet through his eyes and his words, he has been blessed with a penchant for art that empowers us to find serenity and hope in the midst of darkness and despair. The beauty that arises from this imagery, sparked by his own internal struggles, is a tremendous tribute to the true glory of God. From ashes we rise. I encourage everyone to accept James' inspiring invitation into his heart and soul through such a poignant publication."

—Lou Toni, M.D.

"James Cartee, as both a poet and an artist, molds honesty with beautiful imagery to create meaningful reflections on both the deepest lows and greatest joys of life to which anyone can relate!"

—Elizabeth Wiebe, Christian Alliance for Orphans
Vice President of Engagement

"James L. Cartee, III takes us on his journey with this book of poetry. From the death of a loved one to the rejection of a girl in grad school to betrayal by his employer to his descent into depression to the recognition of God's perfect plan when Lisa enters his life. We rejoice in his love of her and his growing faith in God as his life changes to recognize not only his love for his 'special angel,' but his realization of God's work in his life and the work he must do for God as a result. James's imagery and honesty about his feelings and experiences connect to the reader and point the reader to God's plan for his own life."

—Diane E. Tatum, Author,
Speaker, and Educator

"Good poetry brings out the emotions of the reader. Great poetry puts you into the actual emotions of the writer. James L. Cartee, III accomplishes this feat with stunning success, where you actively feel what it is like to know his heartbeat and stand in the shoes of his soulful words. Hence the way he describes his future wife in 'Raindrops Against My Cheeks,' is ultimately how we all want to experience love but are unable to often express our emotions with the elegance that Cartee achieves here. If you want to see love and loss defined in their deeper meanings, then naturally you would want to buy and read this anthology of poems. With a text that brings clarity to anyone's life, you will surely wear a few tears on your shirt sleeve with many of the poems as his life's reality becomes your own."

—Brandon Croom, Esq.,
Lawyer and Military Officer

CONTENTS

FOREWORD

When I was first asked to write this foreword to James' fourth major work of poetry, I admit I was worried. What if I read it and then hated it? What if it creeped me out? What if I was later haunted by auditory hallucinations of James declaiming his verse in the dreaded "poet's voice" of unnatural inflections and agonizing poetry slams? What if I needed to report him to the authorities? Yes, I have a vivid imagination—and a long memory.

I mean, over my life in performance, the arts, and periods in higher education, I've suffered through a lot. I've seen versions of The Wiz that had all the animation of atonal corpses. I've judged anti-talent competitions that made me feel like any ability I had was being leeched away. I've played Memory from Cats with youthful orchestras possessing great enthusiasm—and not one lick of talent. I've read short stories and poems that have made me wish that I lived before the written word. I have slowly chewed a notebook while feigning enthusiasm for a Battle of the Emo Bands. Don't get me started on the craft shows from my childhood with my artist mother— my therapists have assured me that even ECT couldn't eradicate those memories.

So yes, I was worried when I was asked. Haven't I suffered enough?

Filled with trepidation, I read. It's neither hateful—though there is anger, nor creepy—though there is darkness. There is also hope, and love, and caring and pain and joy. There's God, and then there's Batman. Yes, there are superheroes—and even supervillains. There's even a heroine.

James' work is broad in its references. He's drawing from Scripture and popular culture, from personal triumph and very personal tragedies. The work is universal in the fact that it is so highly personal—I think every reader can access the joy in an impending marriage, the nostalgia of budding romance, and the anger of professional setbacks. You don't need to be devout to find his devotion appealing, nor a comic-book or movie geek to get the hero of the story.

It's a collection of emotional snapshots—the good, the bad, and the ugly. And through his poetry, James allows you to experience all three. You are invited to read for yourself—and perhaps you'll feel the same feelings of wistfulness, vindication, joy, and sadness. But throughout all, I hope you see the connection James is feeling—to his faith, his love, and his history.

—Eric A. Hauser, Ph.D.

PREFACE

This poetry book is both about hardship and falling in love, specifically with Lisa Ciuffetelli, who is now my wife. With her name now changed, Lisa Joy Cartee serves as the inspiration for why my fourth major work of poetry culminated into this small anthology in only one year, whereas my previous poetry and photography books took multiple years to filter through draft after draft of continuous edits. I was motivated by Lisa, through our growing relationship, to write and write and write. It has been another awesome journey to see these poems develop into my own present emotional existence.

While I thank the same individuals time and time again with each book that I compose, I constantly appreciate the support of my family, Leslie Stobbe, Wally Turnbull, Betty Turnbull, Dr. Eric Hauser, my Word Weavers writing critique group, the individuals who have endorsed this book, Teri McLaren for her artwork on the book cover, and anyone who has encouraged me to become better: both as a writer and a person.

God introduced me to Lisa, and as such, I will always be grateful for the online dating service that brought us together and the love that continues to flourish as time moves forward. God does, indeed, work in mysterious ways. Thank you, Jesus!

This book contains messages of depression, love, hope, and dark places. It is about emotions and how they influence us as people daily, our hearts and our souls. This compilation serves to show that Christians experience the same negative and positive feelings in all situations, including the false belief that we stand alone against adversity. Individuals can choose to live amongst community and meaningful relationships. The truth is we are not alone and never were.

When we are broken and cannot withstand the threshold of pain any longer, there is hope. God delivers us at that exact moment. There are better days ahead. Sometimes we just need to hear this reminder from another person who has lived in our shoes during similar circumstances. I hope these poems provide that outlet of comparison for you, the reader who might just need some encouragement, in the most desperate and darkest of hours.

*Poetry is when an emotion has found its thought
and the thought has found words.*

—Robert Frost

Raindrops Against My Cheeks

Tens and tens,
Hundreds and hundreds,
I drove to see you
At your Austin door.
Corpus Christi and Nashville
Could not keep me
From falling down on knees
At your beck and call.
I will be loved
As you continue to wonder
About our future,
Solidified in a drive
Of the pouring raindrops
Landing against my cheeks.

Does it really matter anymore?
We are deeply in love.
I sought you, the girl
With the broken heart.

I plan to spend everyday
With your gracious presence.
You no longer wear
A broken smile
Because our lips
Embrace in the backdrop
Of lightning flashes
Among the serious storms
As we both feel loved.

You no longer fall
Because I knocked

On your door
So that you
Would never
Hurt again.
Hearts soar.
No more misery.
I ended your
Personal continual war.

I am your king.
You are my queen.
The raindrops pour
On my cheeks
As I dance
Round and round and round.
Reality sinks in
As I let go forgiven
Of every water-stained sin.

I look for you, the girl
With a heart full of scars.
We share each moment
From here forward
As I make you feel
Forever beautiful.
While we are loved
And further given the grace
To love one another
And never say "Goodbye,"
I chose you.
Yes, I chose to fight
And stand by your side.

8/3/16

When Our Eyes Meet

Our eyes glance across the room.
My heart skips a beat,
Not knowing what to do.
I cannot stop staring at you.
Butterflies fill my stomach.
Hamsters turn the wheels
In my crazed mind spinning.
What's your name?
My friend mentions Lisa.
I imagine your pleasant demeanor
Laying on my chest
While watching a movie
Waiting to make my move.
Trying my very best
To fashionably dress
To favorably impress
The girl across the room.
Every guy here
Is thinking the same thing.
What's your name?
Where you from?
Come on girl,
Tell me what moves
Turn you on.
An Italian model struts
In black high heels and a slim dress.
With my backwards baseball cap
Cowboy boots trotting
Belt buckle from the state rodeo
And tattered torn ragged jeans,
I struggle to say what's up.

Did it hurt when you fell,
When you fell from heaven?
A simple smile at a stupid joke,
Our future begins
With a silly moment
Because I lived up to the dare
To speak to the girl
Across the room.
No one guy had the nerve.
I won simply by trying.
When our eyes met
For the very first time,
I knew she was the one,
My only true companion.

8/25/16

My Better Half

I would describe her
As my better half,
My better mate,
My better person.
While I play the
Part of Eeyore,
She plays Tigger,
Or better yet
Winnie the Pooh.
She is a constant source
Of encouragement
And a constant source
Of affirmation.
And in times of despair,
A constant source of hope.

When I no longer see
The good before me,
She reminds me of who I am
With the positive aspects
Of my life in mind.
She highlights
The good things God gives.
When tired and exhausted,
She asks questions
That make me think.
I try too hard.
I try too much.
Not many humans
Could perform at such a level.

When in the depths of depression,
I survived.
I stayed in touch with the game.
I bounced back.
I could have given up,
But I chose not to.
My better half consoled me.
She comforted me.
And in many ways
She saved me.

8/12/16

Lions and Lambs

Lions and lambs make men
In coming to save our sin.
The Savior resurrects to rise
And relationally links to my demise.
Crucifixion changes history forever
In adversity overcome in every endeavor.
Us versus them no longer exists.
For positive changes amidst
Foreseen challenges in life.
Everyone must overcome strife
Towards a new hopeful start
Even when the world tears apart.
Love cures all fractured feelings.
Long-term affections develop in daily dealings
Involved in our much-needed healings.

3/30/16

Baby Like a Cold Beer

I prefer my women
Like a cold beer.
Whether a blonde, brown pilsner,
Pale ale, or IPA,
I am good with clear hops.
Smooth, tasty, and tall to drink,
I like anything that doesn't think too hard,
Doesn't go too fast,
Doesn't chill too quick.

A beautiful sight makes me thirsty.
While quenching my need,
I drink another to rest,
To watch a good game,
And to relax after a day's work.
The pretty refreshment makes me smirk
Like my baby girl: pure enjoyment.
A good woman is like a good beer.
She is something to savor
And something to appreciate.
The love of a woman is a blessing
Like any moment with a beer.
Memories of community are irreplaceable.
Beer provides excuses for social company
As my lady love stands in my corner.
The simple things in life
Are said to be the best things.
I grab my beer.
I grab my lady's hand.
We remember a shared bliss.
I receive a sweet kiss.

For a brief minute,
It is my beer I no longer miss.
It is her touch.
It is her smile.
With a beer in my hand
And my lady on my shoulder,
I am as happy as a Georgia Peach.
I am the luckiest man in the world.

4/1/16

A Thanks for Moms and Dads

Moms make lunches.
Dads proudly protect.
Parents support children.
God's blessing to kids
Let's be forever grateful.

When we need someone most,
You show up
Often no matter what the cost.
Parenthood pays an ultimate price.
For a lifetime,
They continue to sacrifice.

In joy and in sorrow,
Appreciate the parents we have
Because they may not be here tomorrow.
While sometimes tough,
You formed who I am.
I could never thank you enough.

Sometimes I no longer feel alive.
You encourage me forward
In every talent where I thrive.
You continue to give me more,
Serving my continual endeavors,
No matter what my future has in store.

Moms make lunches.
Dads proudly protect.
Parents support children.
God's blessing to kids
Let's be forever grateful.

8/11/16

We Rise, That Is What We Do

You rise.
That is what you do.
You rise again.

I rise.
That is what I do.
I rise again.

We rise.
That is what we do.
We rise again.

The resurrection of Jesus Christ
Serves as our model
For life inspiration and a reason
To rise in the morning.
Adversity tries to bring down believers
Towards a downwards spiral.
Success rarely occurs
Amidst the center of the tornado
When clouds surface
Like Kansas state skies.
Success follows survival
After the storms pass.

Lightning electric compulsion,
I cannot be stopped.
I am no longer dropped.
I am living on the mountains
In marathons I have topped.
No longer suppressed,
No longer depressed,

I rock steady strut
Across this staged performance.
Fired up with enthusiasm, I rise.
I second that motion. Yes, I rise.
That is what Christians do.
We face the fury of the storm
To dance in the rain
With the daring audacity
To resurrect joyfully
In the most impossible
Situations one ever imagined.

You rise.
That is what you do.
You rise again.

I rise.
That is what I do.
I rise again.

We rise.
That is what we do.
We rise again.

8/25/16

She Ruffles My Feathers, but I Love Her Anyway

We drive each other crazy
But we would be crazier without each other.
It never is easy to leave.
As she sleeps in my favorite shirt,
The memory floods my mind
Like a lighthouse on a leaden shore
In the dark night where oceans cling
To waves in the moonlight.

If I were a rooster crowing
In the early morning hour,
There would be one chicken
That ruffles my feathers
And makes my mind wander
To the ledge of the cliff as I jump.

In the insane moments,
I would not change one thing
Because I love her anyway.
A special woman unnerves me
As I pull my curly hair out
To the frenzy of her Italian ways.
We slam the door in frustration
But then rush to embrace
Like fireworks exploding on the 4th of July.

We will always ruffle our feathers
In the dazed love craze
That flirts with insane flavor
With feelings that I forever remember
And continually savor.

8/8/16

Glimmer of a Friend's Hope

We meet randomly on a break from training.
Doubt in my mind continues raining.
I am banging my head against the wall
With all this constant screaming.
My mind unravels with the voices constantly speaking.

A friend gives a brief moment to listen.
With years of experience he hears my concerns.
"I have been there. I certainly know how you feel."
His words settle into my heart and my broken mind.

A calmness surrounds my weary soul.
Sometimes we just want someone to listen,
To understand,
To reciprocate how we feel.

The burden to bear carried on someone else's shoulders.
Ours becomes lightened
Because someone took time to hear us
When we were frightened.

Sometimes the best words are those unspoken
When our hearts constantly remain broken.
The glimmer of hope comes from silent responses
When any friend takes a minute to listen
With the best of empathetic intentions
By giving their undivided attention.

8/12/16

My Number One Fan

I met my special one
With San Antonio skies bright above us.
I never knew she would later
Become my best friend
And my number one fan,
But God had a plan bigger than me.

She builds me up when I am down.
She encourages me
When low spirits beat the best of me.
She affirms me
When I do not believe in myself.

She is my better half.
She is my best friend.
She is my number one fan.
She serves and sacrifices
For those she loves.
I could not ask for a better partner.

I cannot wait to spend my life with her
Because she always cheers me on,
Because she always has so much fun,
Because she is my special lady,
Because she is my only one.

8/14/16

Marble Falls

Marble Falls became my favorite destination.
We spent the weekend growing closer
Than moments experienced before.
You continue to open my world
To new adventures and higher heights.

I will support you through every dream and endeavor.
The journey began with a bang
Like a space rocket launch to remember
As we move closer to our wedding date in October.
We fast forward to our future
As we remember the memories
Of good times in Marble Falls, Texas.
Art galleries, main street coffee shops, lakeside walks,
Longhorn Caverns, and Motel 6 moments.
We celebrate three years together
Eventually to the point of engagement.
My birthday commemorates our wedding
That will soon come to seal our fate.
We buy bolo ties, Christmas jewelry for relatives,
Ice cream cones, freshly made lemonade,
And sweet kisses of your berry lip gloss.
We get up early to see the sunrise.
We finish dinner early to see the sunset.

With the beginning and end of each day,
I fell in love with Marble Falls
And for the girl who traveled this trip with me.
Lisa makes the most of our weekend away
With every sunrise, with every sunset,
In her arms I wish to relax and stay.
We were clearly made to be together
For every single second of every single day.

7/19/16

Meaningfully Connect

Stuck in a blessed bore,
Step by step the process defines me.
Community with relationship brings more.
The roots connect my life's family tree.

Hope in quality seeks to improve.
Drowning as I seek to float,
I question if this is the right move.
I am tempted to jump the boat.

Monotony adds to the routine of seven days.
Jonah ran to sink in the belly of a whale.
He wanted his own instead of God's ways.
I won but feel like I continue to fail.

I wonder why I continue to care,
The theme of this life seems so unfair.
I fight myself in the mental papers I tear.
Finding peace within seems extremely rare.

Cowboys giddy up into the sunset.
Sailors catch sea creatures late into the night.
Like Jonah, I continue to fret.
While I seek to control destiny, I want to be right.

Jonah let go to give into God's Will.
He stopped running fast away.
He gave up and let go to God's deal.
I listened so that I finally decided to stay.

I then only experienced the peace of my own reality.
My plans never worked in strategies I created.

I took on an attitude of gratitude mentality.
"Give your life to me," God continually stated.

Enjoying the moment, my adventure finally begins.
The endowment of dreams and gifts flows.
I gave myself up to God to forgive my sins.
In the present, my seed develops roots and grows.

3/31/16

The Knight Rises with James Cartee

Do you bleed?
Because you will.

With one percent chance
That you are the enemy,
I will save all of humanity.
While odds stack against me,
The Dark Knight rises
While I live to my maximum potential
As James Cartee.
The kryptonite breathes
Through collapsed lungs.

You're not brave.
Men are brave.
With courage to defeat
The outsider visiting alien,
I am on defense
For the survival of men.
At the point of your death,
You scream, "Save Diana."
What does that mean?
Why did you say that name?

The heart of every boy
Is a mother's love.
We fight for her.
We would die for her.
I realize we both were conned.
I apologize
And avenge forward

Where wrongs
No longer make something right.
The Knight is here,
And the Evil One
Now has much to fear.

7/9/16

I. —Engagement

Love does not consist
Of gazing at each other
But rather looking forward together.
I want you to grow old with me.
The best is yet to come.
Two hearts mend together.
Two lives begin fresh forever.
As we plan our wedding,
The days ahead become bright.
The paths open up to us.
We are filled with rushing
To get all plans accomplished,
But we take some time out
From the fuss and frustration
To focus on the Lord
And our affections for each other.
The two of us remain grateful
In this most blessed of times.
Remember these moments pass quickly,
And the days will flee from us.
We must never forget
The love we now feel
In its precious remembrance.
An engagement stands as our first step
On the path to man and wife.
We start anew.
We will enjoy each and every day.
We hold each other's hand
And will never lose our way
As we focus on the angels above
With protection that lasts
For all eternity.

6/11/16

II.—Elopement

I elope in October leaves falling.
The sunset breaks on the edge of dawn's
Landscape catching its second wind.
We took our risk to chance
In the midst of this societal romance.
Never be upset, disappointed, or mad.
We were made for each other.
Love came in the aura
Of a country chapel
Surrounded by the love of family and friends.
The cloudy horizon carries a photograph
Of the inspiration found in your oceanic eyes.
You waited over the bridges of time
Before you could say I was yours
And you were mine.

Dragonflies direct my heart,
Coupled with yellow grass
And red leaves falling
In the background autumn season.
My night's bonfire
Reveals shadows in the night to come.
For a while we kept it low key
Until the moment I was no longer forgone
To take it to the next level
With Cupid's arrow plunging
Into the ring of an engagement.

My future is no longer bleak
Where every drop of blood
Seems to leak

From the pain of heart's
Past troubles and challenges.
Underneath my rebirth,
I become a new creation
Where I no longer exist as one.
My clenched fists shatter
The glass ceiling
Where limits no longer
Hold me back
To discover and pursue
My full potential.
With a team member, soul mate,
Forever sidekick, and wife,
I elope into the future
Where picture frames grasp
Our future intakes
The hope together we make.

My heart no longer fights
To stay alive
Because I took the leap
Over the red canyons below
To overcome storms abounding.
I found the solid pillar
These tornados could not crumble
Because with this partner by my side
I will no longer stumble.
With the strength of God together
We found hope inside of each other.

6/12/16

III.—Marriage

Growing old together,
We take our vows beyond elopement.
In the journey of this life,
We found each other as partners.

The feeling of missing you grows too strong.
I need you desperately standing by my side.
I know my moment will soon come
When our lives join and I marry you in May.

It will never get too old to hold your hand
Or walk through the beaches, toes stuck in sand.
We will watch movies late into the night.
You will still love me when I am a morning grouch.

In marriage we will face the world as one.
We plan to start that family of five together.
Every day and every night,
I look forward to the stare of your beautiful eyes.

Thankful I discovered my angel to be,
The one who will raise my children.
In the midst of a downwards spiral,
I found unexpected love at the turn of a corner.

I was already gone,
Ready to cliff dive from the earth's edge.
Running away might have made a good story;
However I must finish this race for God's glory.

Here I stand with our wedding moment:
To marry two people very much in love.
Sometimes more than I am able to show,
You are so special, more than you may ever know.

My heart cries like howling wolves into the night
When you leave me in the distance so far.
You are now my church, high on love;
This is no coincidence. Only faith remains.

You lean into my strong shoulder.
You become my support and aid.
We would die for each other
And go forward to any length.

For once in my own life, I feel happy
With joy that overflows in abundance
Like a Polar Express with untapped optimism.
Nothing can stop this marriage train.

We stand at the alter with a minister
To say the spoken special words:
"I do."
Girl, my heart is on fire, yes, on fire for you.

On the tailgate of a country truck
In the background with Nashville music
Cowboys kick.
Cowgirls slick to the boot-scoot-boogey.

A reception follows
With merry drinks, dances, and treats.
My plane of hope takes off
When you promise to stay forever.

You commit to become my wife.
You commit to join me together in this life.
You stole my heart when you said, "Yes"
In the beauty of that green dress.

I fell for you in the chapel's steeple.
Let's get married.
Let's start this life together.
Let's begin this new adventure.

6/12/16

Depressed But Still Determined

Like searching through a desert
For water while thirsty,
I trudge through my journey.
Down but still determined,
I scale the sand dunes once more.
Like mountain ranges,
I rise to the challenge.
Still in His Presence,
God gives me unconditional love
And patience to keep going.
I roam through my mind
With contemptuous thoughts
To doubt, analyze, and hope.

Perseverance pushes through.
The harder the difficulty,
The more satisfaction in triumph.
I climb the cliffhanger that never ends.
My fingers slip as chalk dries up.
My muscles ache without relief.
I stay the course to finish my pace
As I endure past a marathon
With my obsession to persevere
Beyond my own perceived
Psychological constraints to quit.

Through peaks and valleys,
My burdens I continue to bear
So God teaches me to grow.
Eventually the depression passes
Because my determination outlasted
The doubts looming within.

4/6/16

Focused Forward to Stay the Course

Trapped in the traditional institutions
Of my worst mental trials,
I see my enemy in the mirror
That halts my progress forward.

Stuck in the boredom of a new routine,
I still hold in confidence
Of what I know to be true.
Doubts of my decisions surround me.
Depression chokes my heart
Where I no longer dream,
Where I no longer wish for more,
Where my beliefs become stagnant.
I pray for the hope that I seek.
Light peeks through the shadows.
God reminds me to be patient.
Waiting requires time to sit still
In the silence of spoken visions.

The Holy Spirit shows up
When we least expect it.
Hope will come.
Try to still believe.
Something better lies around the corner.
The journey continues forward.
He determines our steps.
Trust in faith
For God knows your plan.
In this necessary truth,
Find your needed inspiration.

3/29/16

Hope That Rises

Strings pluck my heart
In the orchestra that opens the night.
Fresh air from blue skies
Fills my lungs.
Sunshine rays through open clouds
As warmth caresses my face.
The baseball diamond at night
Illuminates a field at twilight
Before sunset signals
The conductor to begin.
Strings raise up their bows.
Woodwinds whistle.
Brass instruments blow horns calling
For the beginning of the performance.
Crowded spectators sit edged on seats
In expectation to hear
The best sounds Corpus Christi offers.
Ocean waves crash against rocks.
Seagulls soar above.
The bridge plays a backdrop of beauty.
Song and dance fill a wonderful evening
Of familiar classical tunes.
Fireworks conclude a memorable occasion.
Colors shoot off like rainbows,
And diamonds shine like midnight stars.
A silhouette glimmers from afar.

On one knee bended,
In the shadows,
I propose an engagement
With ring in hand.

Tears flowing from her eyes,
She quickly says, "Yes."
We kiss passionately
Like a quartet on concert tour.
The symphony plays a high tune
In its grand finale.
As fireworks explode,
The announcement is clear.
Hope rises in this union.
We are getting married.

3/29/16

July 5th in Austin, Texas

After an amazing Fourth
With family so close,
So welcome,
So inviting
Toward strangers.

Kindness
Open doors
And a sister
Who hugs
And loves on me.

Together
Next to your side
Is not close enough
For me
Separated by inches
I declare
"Marry me."

I ask the question
At the Vulcan statue
With a sunset
In background
Glimmering
In your radiant
Eyes with tears
Running down.

Today
As I finally
Reach the nerve

To propose
And change
My life everlasting.

I travel to Austin
In transition
To a new life
With you.

Never long enough
A week passes
Forget the world
As time moves.

No more shame
No more guilt
Confidence
Bursting forth
You marry me
In an October
Country chapel
At Tannehill Park.

Say "Yes."
Say "I will."
Say "I do."

You wear white.
I wear black.
You captivate me
In a dress
So eloquent
The angels sing
In celebration
With a union

God predestined
Since our birth
And creation.

I stand inspired
Because my wish
Fulfilled true
So I could
Say to you
"I do."
Marry me.
Be Mrs. Cartee.
Say "We will."

I walk across
The Austin airport
To throw my arms
Around my fiancee
To embrace my future
To embrace my wife.
Weights lifted
No longer needing
To search.
I finish the race.
Marry me.
The wait is over.
We do.
We will.
You are eternally
Gracious
And beautiful.

7/5/16

Let Go to Trust Him Again

In the midst of transition to a familiar land,
I struggle to let go and trust God.
New and still known to this homecoming,
I am grateful to experience a new part of the journey.
Family and friends support a fearful anxiety.
New to an unchartered workplace society,
Worries consume me with panic in sleepless nights.

I pray next to my bedside
On my knees
With tears of joy
Because God teaches me to let go.
Amidst my own internal turmoil,
I learn to trust again. I learn to trust again.
Lord, please teach me to let go
So my trust becomes natural within my very being.

3/25/16

Love That Transforms

She brings forth selfless pursuits
In expressions of love that transforms
Me into a new creation.

With a fresh start,
Each day renews my strength.
I seek new measures
To challenge myself.

But I still work meaningless matters
In the waking of a new dawn.
I stare at the sunshine
Caught in the perils of survival mode.
Is this routine what others settle for?
They work in boredom
Only to pay bills!

Dreams stand still in a trip
That closes in on foot
Where hands claw for new spaces.

I am defeated only to rise again
In the reminder of a resurrection
That I am forgiven of all sins.

I find hope amidst
The dreary dullness of another day.
I seek God in profound ways
Because of the sacrifice paid.

Fearfully and wonderfully made,
I look forward to better days ahead
Where I no longer feel dead
Where significance is found in,
In all things said.

3/28/16

Steady Hearts

She is loving in many ways
In spite of my bad days.
She still stays sassy.
She remains hopefully passionate,
Inspired to be better,
And motivated to become more.
She uses her God-given gifts
For us
For the future
Even when we disagree.
The prayers move forward
Exchanging our woes for wishes.
Living in the moment,
There is so much to be grateful for
In our new life together.

3/30/16

No Excuses, No Explanations, Just Do It

You offer lame excuses
Lame explanations.
I tire of laziness.
I tire of blaming others.
I tire of selfish guilt trips.
It makes me sick.
About you,
About your time,
About your longing
To belong.
Get over yourself!
As Exodus demands,
Move forward already.
Move on. Move along.
Let's go!
Stop with the pity party
And just do it.
No further excuses.
No further explanations.
Just do it!

7/9/16

Allison, Her Name Never Ends

We were raised
Like a Brady Bunch couplet
We were so close
And always got along.

Like two peas in a pod,
We could not be separated
In the sandbox,
On the soccer fields,
And at Poppi's farm.
You held my hand
As I held yours.
Divisions between us
Were rare if ever existent.
Against any potential bully,
Your fist stood ground
In defense of your little bro.

I admired the shadow
Of my older sister
In the steps that she walked.
I admired her
Because she was my hero.

I will never forget the night
A phone call came
Where I heard news
About the accident
That would change
My life forever.
A presence
Now absent

Longing to see again,
No void could fill the hole
In my weary soul.

The rain poured.
The windshield smothered,
And she could not see five feet
In front of views too close
For one's own good.

On the bends
Descending down Lookout Mountain.
One curve swings over the next.
A fishtail of rain torrents
Reaches through the fog
To pull the car out of control.

The guard rails
Cannot keep the automobile
At bay with a safe impact.
The car blasts
Like a rocket
Off the platform
Into spaces unknown.

Ashes hit the ground.
Steam rises from the burnt engine.
Oil seeps through the dirt.
The wrecking ball
Smashes glass.
Wrapped around a tree,
You wrecked me.

The airbags deployed
But no longer mattered.
Her head knocked
The ironclad steering wheel
With the force of a bullet.
It was too late.
It was all too sudden.

A week later we would mourn.
A week later we would wear black.
A week later we would
Say our goodbye's one last time.

Bryan left a single father.

James left a single brother.

No pain serves to express
This impossible dream.
I awake in sweat
To a nightmare no longer lived
But reality still sets in.
She is gone.
I am without.
My arms no longer climb.
My legs no longer run.
I stand in shock
Looking out at skies
From the place of the wreck.

Tears stream down my face.
No one can ever
Take her place
In my heart.
Oh, how my life would change.

Oh, how my life did change
That night
In the midst of an accident
In tragedy that we never overcome.

She sleeps on her way to heaven.
We never forget her smile,
Her love,
Her motherhood,
Because she was my life,
My shooting star,
And my best friend.
Her life never ends
Because she now rests
In God's hands
For all eternity
Forevermore.

As long as I am with you,
There is no place I'd rather be.

6/13/16

And Then I Knew

I spent most of my life
Searching for the one.
I remember the city
Where I first met you
For the anniversary
To remember
Whose presence changed
My whole world.
I cannot believe
The time that passed
Thus far.
I knew I loved you then
For the future forever.
I can see my babies
On the way
Until we grow old
With a 50th anniversary.
Grandkids celebrated
With birthdays
Into our progressed age.
My continual existence,
All my emotions,
My entire reason for living.
I remember to say
I remember then
That we were meant to be.
I no longer looked
I no longer searched
To see where she might be.
I found her
Sitting in San Antonio,
Sitting right in front of me.

7/5/16

The Angel in the Wedding Dress

With the first dress we choose,
She slipped into memory once again.
I try to keep my thoughts clean
But beauty instinctively brings features
Into silhouetted focus.
I remember the white threads
For what photographs cannot justify.

You dance around in circles
As your dress swirls
Around your natural beauty.
You wear a cream white
Dress with a gossamer veil
That highlights your
Long kobicha shiny hair.

The wait is finally over.
The wedding is near
To marry me and my family.
Diamonds hold your veil
In place to still show
The twinkle of your eye
And the grin of your dimples.

Simple flower and spring patterns
Line your waist and breast
To glorify your figure.
So our song plays in the background.
The harps pluck strings.
The angels sing hymns
At the sight of this heavenly being.

At first I saw the earthly angel
As I said "Hello"
In a museum café.
My heart shifted
As the future lifted
A wedding dress to marry me,
To marry me.

The veil showers raindrops
Upon your shoulders
As laced shoulder straps
Wear out the words
"I love you."
In the stunning breaths
I lose to grasp,
You promise to be
Happy forever by my side,
But forever seems so short.

Diamonds and pearls
Cover your elegance
To the bottom of your figure
Where accents of beauty shine.

Rusty cowboy boots make
Your dress complete
In a Nashville ceremony
Where tears flow down
Uncontrollably at the sight
Before my sore eyes
That cannot believe I am here.

The beauty stands before me
In the transformation
Where two finally join to one.
My heart promises to sing to you
As the music never dies.
The celebration rings through the night.

You remind me
That God keeps his promises
As we look into each other's eyes.
Marry me as we face the future,
As we clinch hands
Where side by side
Could never be close enough for me.

All the audience stares
At the gorgeous sight before us
You in that white dress.

The center of attention,
I had the nerve to say, "Hello"
In that San Antonio café
To eventually ask you to marry me.

On bended knee,
You hesitate with an answer
To say a squeaky, "Yeeessss!"
The angel in the white dress
For a future memory
Agrees that we will be married.
We will be married.

8/8/16

Into My Soul

I long for the peace of His presence.
I long to feel the power of the Holy Spirit.
I pray He intervenes on my behalf
To protect my future
For the hopes of promises fulfilled.
I stand exposed to outside elements.
All negative factors surround me.
They strangle me without pause,
Without break, without a momentary release.
I drown from unseen forces
That inject poison into my veins.
I ask God when this trial will end.
I desire death over life when every moment
Intrudes on my will to continue forward.

I cry to my God, "Why have you forsaken me?
Oh, my God, why have you forsaken me?"
I listen with tears rolling down my cheeks.
He finally answers, "I am here.
Do not be anxious. Do not be afraid.
For I am here. I heard your pleas
For my intervention with matters of the heart."

As I lean into the shoulders of His love,
Slowly I feel comforted and lightly refreshed.
God restores when our nerves can take no more,
When our legs are about to give,
God delivers us with His mercy
Just in time before our collapse.
God paid the price so we no longer would have to.

Peace finally settles upon me.
I breathe and ease into a deep settled sleep.
I let go of what only He could control
Because I listened as God spoke quietly into my soul.

8/20/16

Spiral Fractures in Good Fortunes

My arm shatters into seventeen pieces.
Chess moves of life bring cold traces.
I am a boy, caught in frenzied races.
The dark mindset defines me
In my adolescent days
I withstand adverse nightmares
To much of my own demise.
As a boy, I long for her
With a support system in place.
Through two accounts
Of downwards spirals
And two more accounts
Of wild highs,
I search from ocean to ocean,
Island to island,
Beach to beach,
Mountain to mountain,
Hill to hill,
Five hundred miles,
And one thousand more.
I fall apart in the effort to control
Until letting go in the moment I rise.
An angel falls into the dreams
Of a new fateful resurrection.
I once again find my inspiration.
She arrives to create a new generation.
The search ends. Life begins.
I survive to tell my story
Because together in marriage
We bring God His desired Glory.

3/29/16

Lack of Focused Control

Can I control it?
No, it was beyond me.
Did I cause it?
No, the cause I could not foresee.
Can I cure it?
No, illness sometimes just comes to be.

If the answer remains "No,"
Give the matter to God
And be certain to know
That we only grow
When we realize
That we must
Just let it all go.

3/28/16

In My Most Desperate Hour

In my most desperate hour,
I feel lost.
Like an Israelite
In the desert,
I search for water
But find no source.
I pray to God
With many pleadings
And wonder if He listens.
My family and friends
Try to boost my morale,
But I still suffer
In the silence of misery.
Constantly exhausted and tired,
I no longer wish to endure.
My adversity seems unsurmountable.
Each step forward seems
Harder than the one before.
I hit the floor hard,
Unable to pick myself back up.
Down thoughts steal my joy.
Long-lasting happiness feels
Like a far-removed reality.
I wish for it to end
Because I can no longer
Bear the burden.
I let go of the edge
As I slip away
To fall down below
And experience the peril
That awaits me.

8/12/16

The Goal, Not the Timeline

Danger lies behind scenes
When you focus on the timeline
Rather than just the goal.
The timeline takes
Longer than planned
Causing us to lose sight
Of the mission at hand.
Our vision is not just a timeline.
Our vision becomes
The accomplishment in sight.
Achievement defines
Crossing the finish line
No matter how long
One took to get there.
It is the goal itself,
Not the pace.
Endurance carries
One across the threshold.
Once attained
Time never mattered.
Success with the goal achieved
Becomes all that did.

8/19/16

The Guardian of the Sea

I press forward to higher heights to continually advocate.
We never quit to fight for this inspired cause.
To honor God in this manner opens the floodgate.

I am the guardian of the sea.
When you are about to drown,
You can search among the waters for me.

I defend the fatherless, the widow, and the disabled
Because greatness is upon me to serve others
And stand up for those bullied and falsely labeled.

I grow sick of those who take advantage of the weak
However I am not easily deceived
By stupidity for those who mock society's freak.

I am a freak in action without fulfilled satisfaction
Where my anger grows like a Hulk
Who turns green toward any wrongdoing in action.

I am on it with God's delivery; he's got my back.
The angels stack the sky behind my stance.
We stand ready for battle to defend any attack.

I hold my hands in the air with experienced victory.
To do the right thing and defend the defenseless,
There is nothing wrong that might be contradictory.

I press forward to higher heights to continually advocate.
We never quit to fight for this inspired cause.
To honor God in this manner opens the floodgate.

7/19/16

The Dark Horse Gallops

The dark horse gallops
Into desperate hours of the night.
I stand in His Glory
Amidst my own tears in twilight.

You will pay a price
For what you have done.
I continue forward in action.
I still sprint to my marathon run.

I thrive in your created intentions
And the process of my pain.
When the beat of angels hit your door,
The revenge in my blood begins to rain.

You tried to conceal your secrets;
I bring truth to your plans of rejection.
Guardian angels heal this disease
As floods pour in your forged infection.

I am a soldier for Christ!
My shoulders hold up under scrutiny.
I throw the tea into the harbor
And resurrect in rebellion of my mutiny.

Say goodbye to Hollywood performances.
The comics close with smirks so smug
Along with the beer and liquor
In hypocrisy of liquids that you drug.

The judge of self-condemnation
Catches up with your consciousness in mind
Over time of skewed standards
You lost your way in the lies you signed.

The dark horse gallops
To claim your murky watered soul.
You buried your body into the ground
With all the lives whose goodness you stole.

8/4/16

When Faith Kicks In

I struggle to squeeze and not let go.
I fail to remove my mind from the vision.
I control until tears of frustration
Flood my eyes.
My heart shifts to
Count on His power
And great provision.
I am right where I belong.
I think to myself
About where my Big God
In the sky sees me scurry
In the hurry that all is up to me.
It's time to loosen this tight grip
And rest in the guided wings
Of a thousand guardian angels.

When impossible for me alone,
That is when faith kicks in.
Dear God, I want to praise you
In my tears where I stand.
I want to let go
Of my own magic band
In the false presumptions
That I govern my own world.
I am confused and exhausted
As to why my best efforts
Never play the tune I long for.
When I praise you
At the weakest of my own volitions,
I then surrender,
And God's wonderful plans

Become known to me.
My faith becomes restored.
I move forward
To the comfort
Of what he predestined for me.

I am not leaving with regrets.
Heaven waits for me.
Oh yes, God's arms wait for me.

8/6/16

The Wolverine Within

On my 34th birthday,
I recall the vengeance I seek.
The blood boils
Within my veins
As the blades puncture my skin.
The Wolverine within
Never forgets the stabbed backs
While turned around
With my shoulders
Stacked against the wall.
My anger screams
Fits of rage
To bring the animal out
To his full development.
Once down this path,
There is no turning back!
Like an army general
With hidden agendas,
You brought out
The worst of me.
Do not be surprised
When I come after you
With all energy expended.
You will be held accountable
For your actions
Taken against me
In the discrimination
That so blatantly occurred.
A lawyer delivers.
The board rules in my favor.
Full of egotistical infatuations,

I catch you off guard
In your overgrown cockiness.
Look at my dust.
Look at my feet shaken.
I am done with you.
While forgiven,
I have not forgotten.
I will not let go
Until you suffer
As I did
In the ground
I bury beneath me
Where your self-righteous
Seed no longer hurts,
Where you no longer
Negatively patronize others.
I am your judge,
And now I have judged
The sins committed
Against so many.
You heard the wrath
Of my vindictive injury.
There will be a lightning
Sound to strike.
The show is over.
My performance ended.
At the end of your survival,
In your dumbfounded finality,
I will conduct the last song
Of this triumphant symphony.

7/19/16

The Hypocrite's Oath

Engrossed by your own sights,
You brainwash those who work
Under your crooked leadership.
With no vision,
As the CFO, you make the CEO decisions.
With no accountability in this organization,
The media will expose your corruption.
I stand in silence, pretending to care,
As you stain the soil with government
Dollar bills in the pockets of gross numbers.
Your message is heard.
Your greed still unfortunately reigns
To the spoils of others hurting.
Vapors of water travel through minds
That worship your every move.
Nothing valiant about your character,
You believe you are powerful
Standing with the elite Alabamian cliques.
Injustice sits at your every move
For the pretender you pretend to be.
Please remember the name.
I feel better to fight.
My name is James Cartee.
The hypocrisy of your organization
Will be exposed in the light of truth.
I dive fearlessly to bring the spotlight
To the door of your deception.
I no longer resist the jealous hate
Because you will also fall
Into this tormented state.

I rise to the orbit of new Saturn rings.
Destiny brings the downfall of your plunder.
In the cold night you shake.
In the cold night you shudder.
I am coming to chop down the tree.
I am coming to stop those who flee.
You messed with the pit bull within me.
You can longer play the hypocrite you are.
You took this game too far.
Now your playhouse burns to the ground
As I stand there and hear the cries
Of every lingering sound.

6/12/16

The Riddick Rebel in Me

You tried to bury the soul within me.
You could not control the demons rising to be.

The Riddick Rebel resurrected to foster new creations.
The hypocrites failed to destroy my heart's inspirations.

The lawyer swallowed hard these obvious said wrongs,
But the playwright continued writing hit songs.

Jump in a river. Drown me until air no longer flows gasping.
Suck the wind out. Hold my throat with your clasping.

In the past, I persevered through much worse
As if powerfully living in a rebellious never-ending curse.

I bluntly expose the hypocrisy of your stated mission.
With fake numbers, long ago you lost your valued vision.

Turn your television up. Listen to media outlets of the world.
Your pretense to preach a better Gospel makes me want to hurl.

What goes around comes around with truth revealed
What you no longer could hide in the lies you concealed.

I quietly sink into my own thoughts of restoration
Knowing I am no longer depressed in captivation.

I rebelled in the face of obvious committed hidden sin.
I rebelled because I am not like your other manipulated men.

My name stands to be remembered as James Cartee,
And you could never kill and bury the man God made me to be.

7/9/16

Never Again Get The Best of Me

Electricity will never again get the best of me.
The shock of my spirit runs deep
As audience members remember my name,
Not the first, not the second, but the third
Knighted James Louie Cartee.
When you listen to the advice of hypocrites,
You then become one of those manipulators
To later look yourself in the mirror
In the realization that you are a hater,
A hater of yourself for crawling down
The mineshaft of depression that kills
Your every fiber and willing desire to carry on.
We must follow our own masterful willingness
To rise on the occasion for our own decisions.
We are only defined as much as we let them in,
Succumbing to self-pity in this disgusting sin.
Men and women think they know best for others
When at some point we must decide for ourselves.
God, oh my God, you are the best support
That a Holy Spirit driven energy has given me.
You live inside with the best of intentions.
We must listen to our inside gut,
To our inner voice, to our natural instinct
To do what we confidently know is right.
Pressed into a corner where I cannot claw out,
Never again will I fight what I know to be wrong.
I will sing the newness of this proclamation song.
I am inspired to be a new creation,
Birthed to begin a new awareness of self.
I prefer present over perfect everyday
Because answers from Him in prayer fulfill

The searching in my soul to simply be still.
Humans will let you down.
Men will disappoint. Women will frown upon you.
There is only one holy entity in the heavens
Whose name we can forever cry for deliverance.
While young, we were not singularly afraid.
We trudged over every mountain,
We sprinted up every hill in front of us.
We swam across every river and every lake.
The Spirit of God lived in us,
And somewhere along the way,
We lost track of our inner strength
Later to only be broken
So that we may find it once again.

9/9/16

Lisa, Not Jenn, The Heat Turns On

You turn,
You turn,
You turn,
Watching
You turn
The heat on.
I am losing it.
My heart yearns
For your sexy burn.

Jenn lost
A chance
To swing
With this
Country
Cowboy.
I asked her
To be
My girlfriend
And future wife.
God turned
You rather
And better for it.
Coming through
A tipsy smile,
I am gone.
No whiskey,
No beer,
No Jack Daniels
Fire.

I stand sober
Inspired
With my body
Hazy.
You put
Your hands on me.
I put my hands
On you
With thirteen
Gray shades
Of heated crazy.
Our bodies unwind.
A perfect twist.
A perfect match.
I will do anything
You want me to.
Jenn screwed it up.
God had a better plan
So that I could
Be your turned on man.

You turn,
You turn,
You turn,
Watching
You turn
The heat on.
I am losing it.
My heart yearns
For your sexy burn.

7/5/16

Steadfast and Not Forgotten

I am steadfast in purpose
With unmet resolutions.
I have not forgotten
Your chosen deeds,
Your chosen wrongs.
Your sin seamlessly
Fades in your past
Only later to be revealed
In structures crashing down.
You never expected
This courageous mold
That you never controlled.
I will not remain silent.
I will not go quietly
Into the night
For the imaginary numbers
You forged to report
For continual funding
In the Judas bag of gold
You accepted in treachery.

I clean out the closet
Of faded skeletons
You never thought
Anyone could resurface.
The governmental entity
Takes a closer investigation.
You never figure me out.
You probably wish
You never met me now.
Ousted for false reasons,
It's time to start a new season.

Your doors close
At your corrupt ways
And your failure
To face and take care
Of your chosen few own.
I walk away with fire
Set by the matches
From my pocket.
I shake the dust
Off my heels.
In the background,
The building explodes
From the gasoline
I poured in the path
Of political agendas
And selfish ambitions.

I am steadfast.
I am not forgotten.
You could not throw
Me away at a funeral
With soil on top of my coffin.
I rose above the judgment
To conflict chaos
In the honesty
Of exposed crime
For your own obligated
Jailed and served time.

8/6/16

I Persist for You

Like bear claws tugging at my flesh,
The depression strangles my throat.
I want to quit.
I want to give up.
I persist for you.
Your memory comes fresh to mind—
Your palm against mine, the caress of your skin,
The touch of your lips, and the stroke of your hair.
The intricate nature of your beauty
Transforms the renewal of my mind.
God sent this angel to deliver me
From the madness of an erratic mind.
While the illness cannot be stopped,
It can be relieved.
It can be confronted.
Persistence in the face of trials
Remains a choice for those suffering.
We choose to press on for those we love.
When I no longer know what to do,
I try my best to think of you.
I persist with those thoughtful reminders
Because you never gave up on me.
So how could I give up on us!
I persist for you.
That is what I have chosen to do.

8/13/16

Lack of Quality Accountability

There is no quality about your assurance.
I took out a life loan in the policy of insurance.
I chased that dream that started off lost.
You dropped me without accountability at any cost.
Knowing I can flow harder than you can,
I worship by the side of this Jesus man.
You advocate for the mentally ill
And make me vomit in my stomach, for real.
I blow hard breaths as the green beast awakes
In all the promises with endless scenes of many takes.
Hypocrites pass by. Hypocrites commit hate crimes.
My vendetta catches you in these gruesome times.
I kill it on the first take to set the pattern strokes
In all the laws you broke in the pain God revokes.
Holy fire falls on your head
To create the stop of something already dead.
You will never terminate again
Because I exposed your lame excuses in sin.
I pray you no longer tame the lion heart of any man
When you toss the paper in the trash can.
I'm done with you.
You will no longer know what to do
When I burn down your little playhouse.
No game waits with this supposed blind mouse.
Ringing your eardrums like a cell phone,
You will never forget the sound of my dial tone.
Accountable you will be held guilty for your action
Until I believe justice is done to my satisfaction.
No longer can I stand by the people you are hating.
I break the rules. I remember your zero percent rating.
You are going down. You are finally done.

You woke this giant. You messed with the Holy One.
No longer able to give your applause,
I start a flame to stand and pause.
I pour gasoline. The fire rises.
You left me dead to my own demise.
Now there is no compromise.
You now drown in the seas of your own lies.

6/12/16

The Proclamation of Freedom

Our souls stand restored
I challenge life to bring its best
Electrified, I fall to the ground,
Floored without further expectation.
Our secondhand instinct sets in
When truth reminds me of who I am.
A man of strength,
A man whose sin is paid for,
A man who no longer has to give anymore.
We are relieved.
We are no longer hard pressed.
For the sacrifice given,
For the perfect example he was living.

I don't owe anybody or anyone a thing
Because of the cross where my Savior hanged.
I stand still in freedom
With my arms held open to receive blessings
Because all guilt, all shame, all regrets
Hung on a begotten tree
Where I loudly screamed his name,
"Jesus, you alone have set me free!"

9/9/16

To Feel Hope Deliver Me Again—Part One

Hope evaporates into thin air.
It no longer fulfills my heart.
Hope abandoned me.
I no longer feel
Its presence around me.
Despair consumes
My every move.
I would do anything
To feel hope again,
To have my energy,
And to believe
I am worthy
Of His guided attention.

8/13/16

To Feel Hope Deliver Me Again—Part Two

While hope seems lost in a distant field,
Faith delivers when least expected.
When life seems bleakest
And you can go on no more,
Hope arrives at your front door.
Your heart feels empty.
Your soul can no longer move forward.
In God's time, hope will come.
Believe me when I say—hope will come.
When in the depths of depression,
Lean on those who love you,
On those who will not give up on you.
I have long experienced the loss of hope.
Family and friends were there to help me cope.
I slid forever into a dry wall.
When I no longer wanted to survive,
Hope appeared. Hope revealed
God has a purpose for me.
God will not give up on me.
When I am about to let go of the last string,
He reaches for my hand.
He saves me from my last fall.
Then hope begins to call.
I am on my way rising up.
God begins to refill my cup.
The hope once missed appears again.
I remember I am saved from my own sin.
Jesus paid the price so I would not have to.
The ultimate source of hope pours in
As I realize I am completely forgiven.

8/13/16